The Science of Noise

Lynne Wright

WAYLAND

Science World

Other titles in the series:

The Science of
Gravity

The Science of a
Light Bulb

The Science of a
Spring

Picture acknowledgements
Wayland Publishers would like to thank the following for allowing their pictures to be reproduced in this book:
Ace/Patrick Blake 5 (top), /Geoff du Feu 22 (middle), /Ray Spence 5 (bottom); Bubbles/Vicki Bonomo 16 (top),
/Ian West 26, /Jennie Woodcock 19 (top); Martyn F. Chillmaid 10 (both), 28 (top), 29 (bottom); Eye Ubiquitous
18, 21 (bottom), /Roger Chester 16 (bottom), NASA 14; Image Bank 23; Getty Images cover [inset top], 23 (top),
/Lonnie Duka 17, /Robert Frerck 27 (top), 29 (top), /Bruno de Hogues 25; /Tom Main cover [inset centre], /Art
Wolfe 22 (bottom); Robert Harding 4 (bottom), /Louise Murray 21 (middle); Image Bank 23 (bottom); Science
Photo Library/Crown Copyright/Health and Safety laboratory 15 (top), /Tim Davis 21 (top), Richard Megna
24; /Dr Morley Read 19 (bottom); Wayland Picture Library cover [main], title page, contents page, 5 (middle),
7–9, 11, 15 (bottom), 20, 22, 26, 27 (bottom), 28 (bottom), /Chris Fairclough 4 (top); Zefa 12.

Editor: Carron Brown
Consultant: Anne Goldsworthy
Concept design: Lisa Nutt
Designer: Mark Whitchurch
Production controller: Carol Stevens
Illustrator: Peter Bull

First published in 1999 by Wayland Publishers Ltd,
61 Western Road, Hove, East Sussex BN3 1JD

British Library in Cataloguing Data
Wright, Lynne
  The Science of Noise. – (Science World)
  1. Noise – Juvenile literature
  I. Title
  620.2'3

ISBN 0 7502 2404 5

Find Wayland on the Internet at http://www.wayland.co.uk

Contents

Where does sound come from?

There are sounds all around us. Listen, right now, where you are. What can you hear? How many different sounds can you hear, and what is making each noise? If you went to another place, would you hear the same, or other sounds? Next time you are in a busy place, such as a shop or town centre, listen to what sounds are around you. If you go into a park or a wood, do you hear even more sounds?

▲ What sounds do you think you would hear if you were near these cows in the country?

◄ What sounds would you hear if you were near this busy road?

Think of all the sounds you can hear, or that you know. Are they all equally loud, or equally quiet, or are they different? Some may be high sounds, or low sounds, or a mixture of both. You may like some sounds more than others. Do you have a favourite sound? Are there any sounds you don't like?

◀ What sounds do you think you would hear in a shop?

▲ What sounds do you think you would hear on this bridge?

◀ What sounds do you think you would hear in a park?

Describing sounds

Sounds can be described as noisy, or musical. Noise can be tiring, or irritating and, if it is very loud, can harm our ears. A musical sound can also be loud but, because it is produced in a different way to noise, it is usually more pleasant to listen to.

▲ What words would you use to describe the sound the dog is making?

◀ What words would you use to describe the sounds this man is making?

What are decibels?

We measure how loud sounds are in decibels. A whisper measures about 12 decibels. A sound of 120 decibels can hurt your ears. A jet engine 30 metres away makes a sound of about 140 decibels.

◀ What words would you use to describe the sea?

You could sort the sounds you hear into different groups such as loud sounds and soft sounds, or sounds made by machines and sounds made naturally. Think of some other ways to sort the sounds that you know.

What words ▶ would you use to describe a lawnmower?

There are many different ways you can make sounds

You could clap your hands, hum, shake or rattle a jar of pasta or twang an elastic band. You could also make sounds by plucking, like a guitar, by banging, like a drum, or by blowing, like a recorder. Are there other ways, such as scraping and rubbing?

Would these sounds have the same volume, or would some be louder or quieter than others? For example, banging a tambourine would make a louder sound than shaking it. Would these sounds have the same pitch, or would some be higher or lower than others? For example, a hand clap may make a higher sound than a drum.

Vibrations

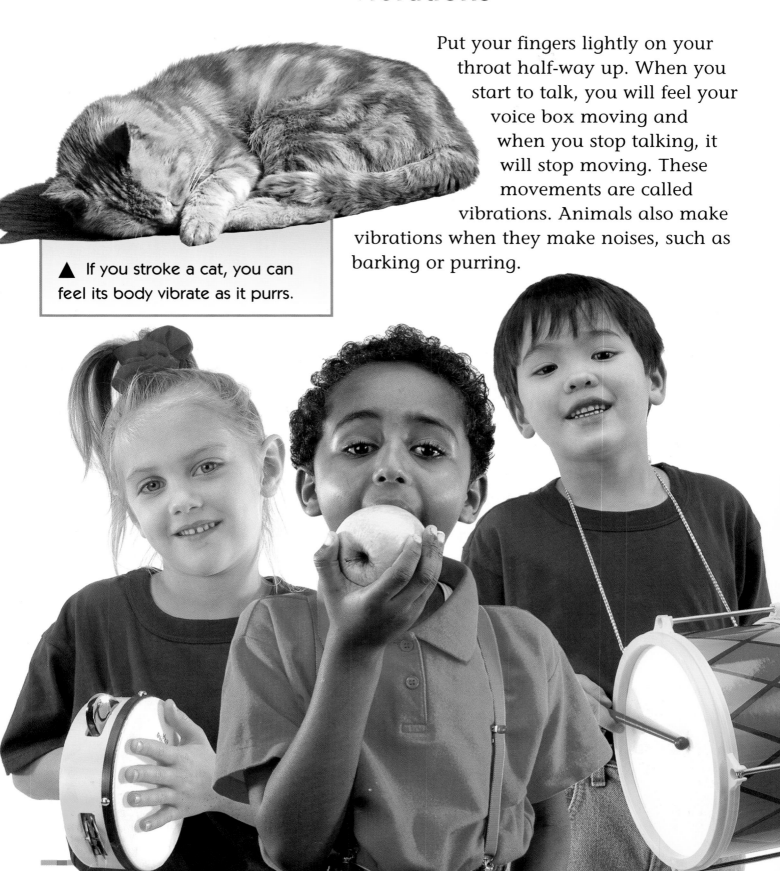

Put your fingers lightly on your throat half-way up. When you start to talk, you will feel your voice box moving and when you stop talking, it will stop moving. These movements are called vibrations. Animals also make vibrations when they make noises, such as barking or purring.

▲ If you stroke a cat, you can feel its body vibrate as it purrs.

What vibrates when you make your own sounds?

How can we be sure that sound is made when something vibrates? Stretch a rubber band across one hand and pluck it with the other hand. We can see and feel the vibrations, and hear the noise.

◀ Hold a ruler flat on a table-top so that most of it is sticking out. It is not moving, and there is no sound. Now bang down on the free end with your other hand. The ruler makes a sound and you can see the free part moving – it is vibrating.

If you put some grains of rice on a piece ▶ of greaseproof paper and hold it above a drum, not touching it, and ask a friend to bang the drum, you can watch the rice grains move. When your friend bangs the drum, the drumskin vibrates. The vibrations flow out into the air around the drum, and start the paper and rice grains vibrating, too.

What happens when you blow across the top of an empty bottle? There is sound coming from the bottle but it is not the bottle that is vibrating, it is the air inside it. If you collect a few identical bottles and fill them with different amounts of water, they will make different sounds.

▼ The bottle with the longest column of air in it will produce a deeper sound than the rest. Which one will produce the highest sound?

What are wind instruments?

Wind instruments are instruments that have one or several tubes of air. A player blows down a tube, the air vibrates and a musical sound is made. There are many different wind instruments, including recorders, flutes, clarinets, tubas and panpipes. All have different ways of making sounds. For example, you blow down a recorder using its shaped mouthpiece, and you blow across the top of a panpipe tube in the same way that you blow across the top of a bottle.

How does sound travel?

An object needs to vibrate for there to be a sound. But how does the sound get from the object to our ears? How do we hear someone clapping their hands across the room?

◄ When we clap our hands, the vibration of the clap makes the air surrounding the hands vibrate. These vibrations travel through the air until they weaken and die away. The vibrations are known as sound waves. These waves ripple outwards in all directions from the vibrating object.

Different objects send out different sound waves. The sound waves vibrate at different rates. The pitch of the sound made depends on the number of vibrations per second. The more vibrations there are per second, the higher the sound.

We hear sounds with our ears. The bit of the ear outside our head is only the start of the hearing chain. It works like a funnel to allow the sound waves to travel down it to the inner ear inside our head. When they reach the ear drum, it vibrates the sound waves along to the inner ear which sends messages to the brain. The brain then works out what we hear.

▼ This diagram shows how sound travels to our ears.

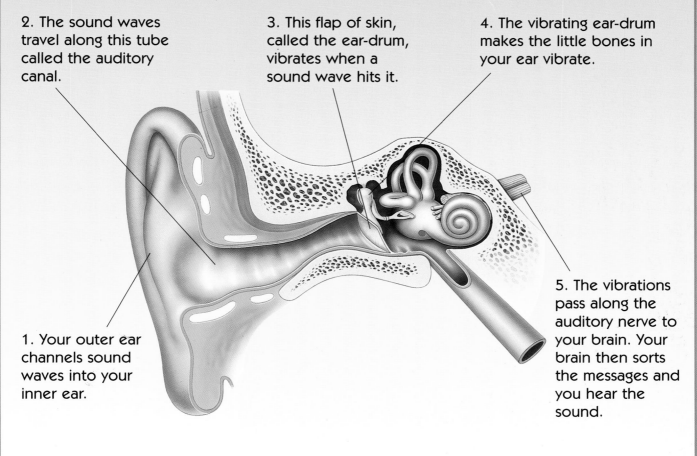

2. The sound waves travel along this tube called the auditory canal.

3. This flap of skin, called the ear-drum, vibrates when a sound wave hits it.

4. The vibrating ear-drum makes the little bones in your ear vibrate.

1. Your outer ear channels sound waves into your inner ear.

5. The vibrations pass along the auditory nerve to your brain. Your brain then sorts the messages and you hear the sound.

Some sounds don't vibrate with enough energy to make our eardrums vibrate, and we can't hear these sounds. Some sounds have so much energy that they hurt our ears. The more energy, the louder the sound.

Does sound only travel through the air?

If you are outside, you hear sounds in the same area you are in or, if you are inside, you hear sounds in the same room you are in. However, you can also hear sounds in other rooms. How do these sounds travel to you if there are walls and doors in the way?

How fast does sound travel?

Sound travels at about 330 metres per second. Light travels almost a million times faster than sound, at 300 million metres per second.

Sound travels through other materials, not just air, so it will travel through the wood of a door and the glass of a window. All materials are made up of tiny bits called particles that vibrate.

◀ In space, there are no air particles and so there is no sound.

Where there is nothing, even no air, there is no sound. This is called a vacuum. Sound will not travel through a vacuum because there are no particles to vibrate.

Sounds travel more
quickly through solid
materials, such as wood,
than through liquids,
such as water. This is
because the particles are closer together in solid
materials. Liquids carry sound better than gases,
such as air, where the particles are spread out
more. Next time you are at the swimming pool
try talking to your friend under water and hear
how loud your voices sound. Is the sound clear?

Ask a friend to tap a table-top with his or her fingers. ▶
Put your head down on the table. Does the sound
seem louder with your head on or off the table?

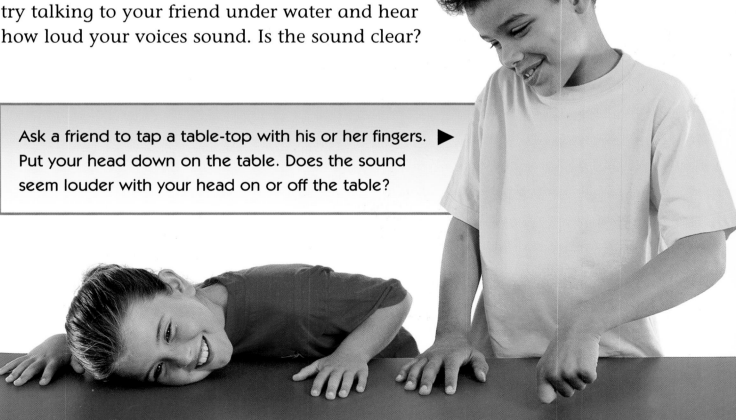

Stopping sounds

Can you think of some times when you don't want to hear anything? When you are trying to go to sleep, you might pull the bedclothes over your ears to block out sounds. If you are concentrating on something you are doing, and you don't want to be disturbed by noise, you might put your fingers in your ears. Doing these things stops the sound waves entering your ears.

Sound travels better through some materials than others, so some materials are better at keeping out the sounds we don't want to hear.

▲ Covering your ears against noise blocks out sounds.

Double-glazed windows are made of two sheets of glass with a vacuum in between them. The sound can't travel through the vacuum and so the room is quieter. Most noise will not travel through, but not all the noise is kept out because sound will travel through the window frames and the walls.

Some buildings near busy ▶ roads, airports or other noisy places have double-glazed windows that stop a lot of the sound coming in from the outside.

Which materials keep out sound best?

The materials that are better at keeping out the sounds are soft ones which contain pockets of air. Since air is not as good at passing on vibrations as solid materials, the sound seems quieter when it reaches our ears.

Some jobs require special ear protection to stop loud sounds damaging workers' ears. You will see people wearing ear protection on building sites, runways at airports and in factories where there are noisy machines.

▼ This carpenter is wearing ear protection while he works to block out the sound of the loud machinery.

Some places need to be especially quiet for a purpose. For example, recording studios and radio stations need to be soundproofed so that outside noises don't spoil a broadcast or finished recording. The walls are made of special materials that keep noise out, and will not cause echoes.

Echoes

Echoes are made when sound reflects off smooth, hard surfaces such as bare concrete, wooden floors and plastered walls. This is one reason we put carpets on the floor, and wallpaper on the walls.

◀ Toys banging on a carpeted floor will be a lot quieter than toys on a solid wooden floor. This is because sound doesn't travel so well through carpets and there are hardly any echoes.

Bats can't see very well in the dark, so why don't they fly into trees and walls at night?

Bats send out very high-pitched sounds as they fly. These sounds echo back from anything in the way of a bat's flight path, so that it doesn't crash. The sounds bats make are too high-pitched for humans to hear.

How do we hear sounds?

We hear with our ears. We have two ears, one on each side of our head, which enable us to say where a sound is coming from. Can you hear sounds equally well that are made in front of you, to one side, or behind you? We can hear round corners and through walls and doors, though we can't always see the places where the sounds come from.

◀ Put something over your eyes and cover one ear. Ask a friend to make a noise behind you. Can you figure out which direction the noise is coming from?

Why is it important that we should be able to hear where sounds are coming from? If we could not do this, we would be in a lot of danger. We could not hear the direction traffic was coming from when we cross the road, or hear where a shout for help came from.

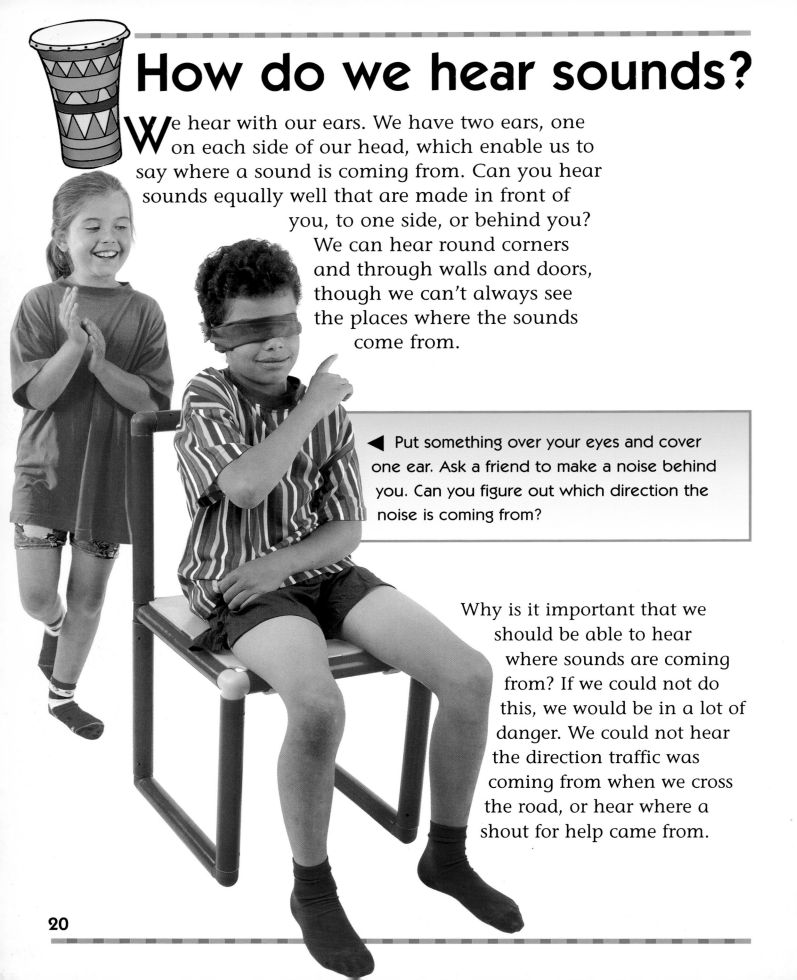

It is very important for some types of animals to hear well. Some animals, especially those that hunt at night, need to be able to listen for their prey. Some animals, which don't feed on other animals, need to hear an animal hunting them.

An owl hunts at night and relies on its hearing to ▶ find its next meal. It hunts small animals, such as mice, and can find one in total darkness just by following a distant sound of rustling leaves.

▼ A lynx uses its good sense of hearing to help it find food.

▼ A rabbit needs to catch the quiet sounds of a hunting animal so that it can escape.

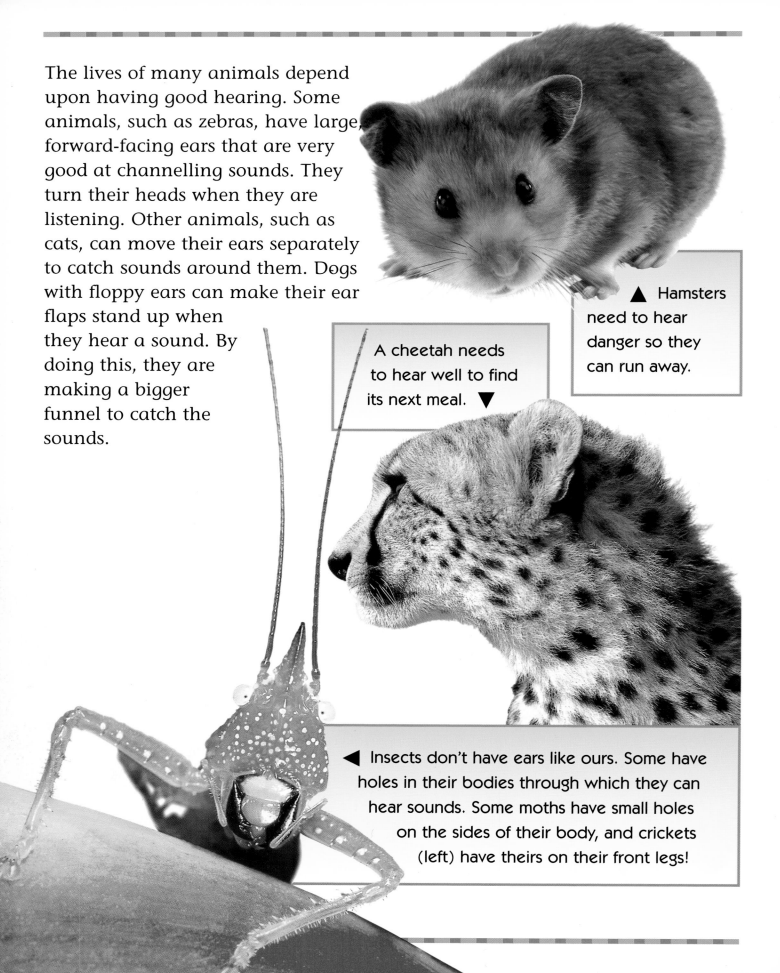

The lives of many animals depend upon having good hearing. Some animals, such as zebras, have large, forward-facing ears that are very good at channelling sounds. They turn their heads when they are listening. Other animals, such as cats, can move their ears separately to catch sounds around them. Dogs with floppy ears can make their ear flaps stand up when they hear a sound. By doing this, they are making a bigger funnel to catch the sounds.

▲ Hamsters need to hear danger so they can run away.

A cheetah needs to hear well to find its next meal. ▼

◀ Insects don't have ears like ours. Some have holes in their bodies through which they can hear sounds. Some moths have small holes on the sides of their body, and crickets (left) have theirs on their front legs!

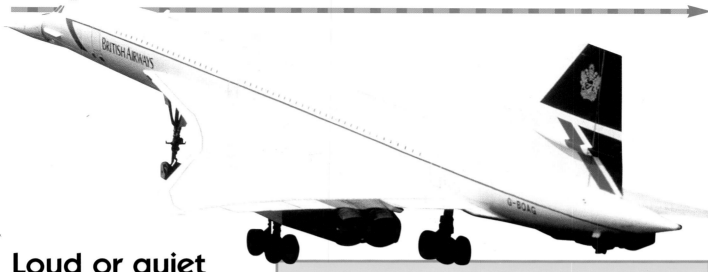

Loud or quiet

If you dropped a pencil tin far away from someone and then near to them, they would hear the sound differently, even though you made the same sound. Sounds seem louder the nearer you are to them. They seem to get quieter the further away you are, even though they really are not. This happens because the sound waves from the vibrating object move out in every direction. As the energy in these sound waves moves outwards and spreads over a greater area, it decreases. Less energy makes a quieter sound.

▲ Concorde travels faster than the speed of sound as it flies across the world's skies. Even though it is hundreds of kilometres in the air, the loud roar of its engines can clearly be heard above all noise on the ground. Loud sounds can be heard further away than quiet sounds because they have more sound energy.

If we want someone to hear us a long way ▶ away, we put our hands around our mouths. This makes a funnel that stops the sound waves spreading so more of the sound energy travels in the direction you want it to.

How can we change sound?

Next time you listen to some music notice how the sounds vary all the time from high to low. We use the word 'pitch' to describe how high or low a sound is. Can you make high and low sounds with your voice? Start with a low-pitched sound and gradually go higher until you are making a high-pitched sound.

The pitch of a sound can be changed. The faster an object or the air around it vibrates, the higher the pitch.

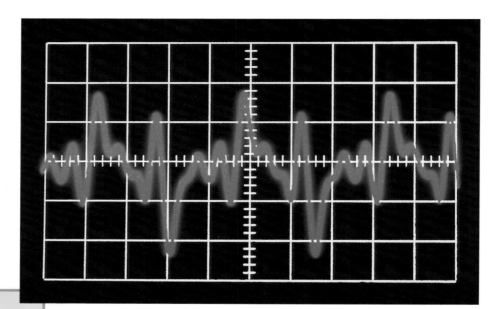

These sound waves ► show the pitch of a note made by a harmonica (top) and a recorder (bottom). The recorder holds a steadier note than the harmonica, shown by the recorder's steady and repetitive sound wave pattern.

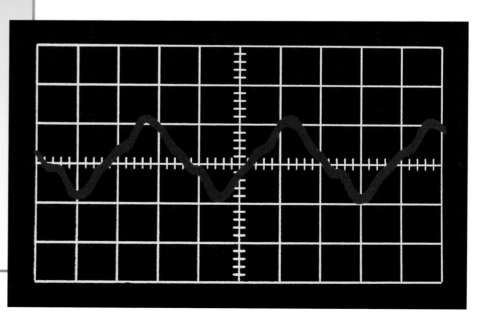

A drum is made of a skin stretched across a hoop of wood or metal. When a drummer bangs the skin with his or her hand, or a stick, the skin vibrates to produce sound. If a drummer only has one drum, he or she could alter the sound it makes by tightening the skin across the hoop. The tighter the skin, the higher the sound.

▲ You can see where the skins of these drums have been secured around the hoop. The drums will all be of different pitch depending on how tight the skin on each drum is.

Stringed instruments, such as guitars and sitars, make sounds when the strings are plucked. If the strings are loose, they will make lower sounds than if they are tight. The pitch of the sounds also depends on where the player places his or her fingers.

This boy is holding a stringed instrument called a ▶ sitar. The strings can be tightened by turning the screws at the top of the instrument. Tighter strings make higher pitched sounds than loose strings.

▼ When this player puts his finger high up on the string, the sound is low-pitched. If he moves his finger down the string, the player will shorten it and the sound will be higher.

Wind instruments produce sounds when the player blows down a tube of air and makes the air vibrate.

◀ Pan pipes have tubes of different sizes and so the columns of air are of different sizes. Which pipe will make the lowest sound? The longest pipe will make the lowest sound. The shortest pipe will make the highest sound.

A recorder is one tube of air with a row of holes down one side. You blow down the tube and cover the holes with your fingers to make a sound. You have to cover different holes to make different notes. This changes the length of the column of air that will vibrate. High-pitched notes are made when you cover one or two holes, creating a short column of air. Low-pitched notes are made when several holes are covered, creating a long column of air.

The player must cover all the holes on the ▶ recorder to produce the lowest sound. How will she make the highest sound?

Varying volumes

Sounds can also be of different volume, loud or soft. The volume depends upon how much energy is put into making the sound. The more energy you put into a sound, by banging, or plucking, or blowing harder, the louder it is.

When you shout, you build up your breath ▶ to let it out in a mighty noise.

▼ When you whisper, you let less breath out and you make less noise. You may also cup your hands around your mouth to direct the sound.

Some stringed ▶
instruments have a box
behind the strings. This makes
the sound louder. We say it
amplifies the sound.

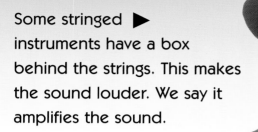

Human ears find very
high and very low
sounds difficult to hear
well. Human ears can detect
sound waves that vibrate up
to 20,000 times a second.

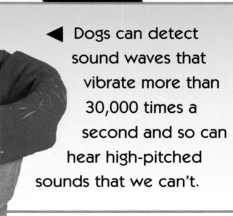

◀ Dogs can detect
sound waves that
vibrate more than
30,000 times a
second and so can
hear high-pitched
sounds that we can't.

29

Glossary

Amplify Make a sound louder.

Auditory Having something to do with hearing.

Auditory canal The inside part of the ear that sound waves are funnelled down from the outer ear. It connects to the ear-drum.

Decibels The units for measuring how loud a sound is.

Ear-drum A flap of skin separating the outside part of the ear from the inner ear.

Ears The sense organs that enable us to hear sounds.

Echoes Sounds that strike a reflecting surface, such as rock, and bounce back so that they seem to be coming from in front of us.

Energy Energy makes things work.

Music A type of sound that is made by an object sending out regular vibrations at regular intervals, such as a guitar string.

Nerve The part of the body that sends messages to the brain.

Noise A type of sound made by an object sending out irregular vibrations at irregular intervals, such as a banging door.

Pitch This describes the highness or lowness of a note, and depends upon the number of vibrations produced every second.

Sound Any noise produced by the vibrations of an object.

Soundproofed Protected against sound. Soundproofing is usually used to keep out unwanted sounds, such as traffic noise, or to stop echoes.

Sound waves Waves of vibrating air that travel through air transferring sound energy from a vibrating object to our ears.

Vacuum A space that has nothing in it, not even air particles.

Vibrations Vibrations cause sound. Different objects and materials vibrate at different speeds. The speed of vibration is measured in hertz (Hz) as the number of vibrations each second. One vibration is equal to one hertz.

Voice box The part of your body where vibrations are produced in order to produce sounds, i.e. your voice.

Further Information

Books to read

Sound (*Fun with Science* series) by Cash Taylor (Kingfisher, 1999)

Sound (*Step-by-Step* series) by Helena Ramsay (Watts, 1998)

Sound, Noise and Music (*Science Workshop* series) by M. Seller (Watts, 1995)

Super Sound (*Science Starters* series) by Wendy Madgwick (Wayland, 1998)

Websites to visit

www.nmsi.ac.uk
The home page of the Science Museum, London.

www.exploratory.org.uk
You can find your nearest hands-on science centre here.

www.frontiernet/~docbob
This site includes many interesting facts on science and technology.

Places to visit

The Science Museum, Exhibition Road, South Kensington, London (Tel: 0207 938 8000).

See websites to visit, above, for information to find your nearest hands-on science centre.

Noise TOPIC WEB

MUSIC
- Listen to different instruments and describe how they sound. Then listen to a piece of music and point out which instruments are being played.
- Look at how the pitch of sounds are changed on different instruments.

GEOGRAPHY
- Visit different areas around where you live and ask the children to describe the different sounds they hear in different places.
- Think about why you hear some sounds louder than others, i.e. because you are near a busy road, airport, etc.

HISTORY
- Look at the design of musical instruments through the ages and why they have changed.

ART
- Listen to a piece of music and paint the patterns you heard, shown by loud spiky lines or soft swaying lines.

DESIGN AND TECHNOLOGY
- Look at how buildings are designed to either stop sound (recording studios) or amplify sound (theatres).
- Look at how different instruments are designed to amplify and play sounds.

DANCE
- Interpret loud and soft sounds in movement and make into a sequence.

SCIENCE
- Explore and investigate everyday noises. Listen to the different volumes and explain why noises are soft or loud.
- Warn about the dangers of loud noises and explain about how people hear differently and how to protect your ears.

ENGLISH
- Listen to a piece of instrumental music and write about what you think it describes.

Index

Numbers in **bold** refer to pictures as well as text.